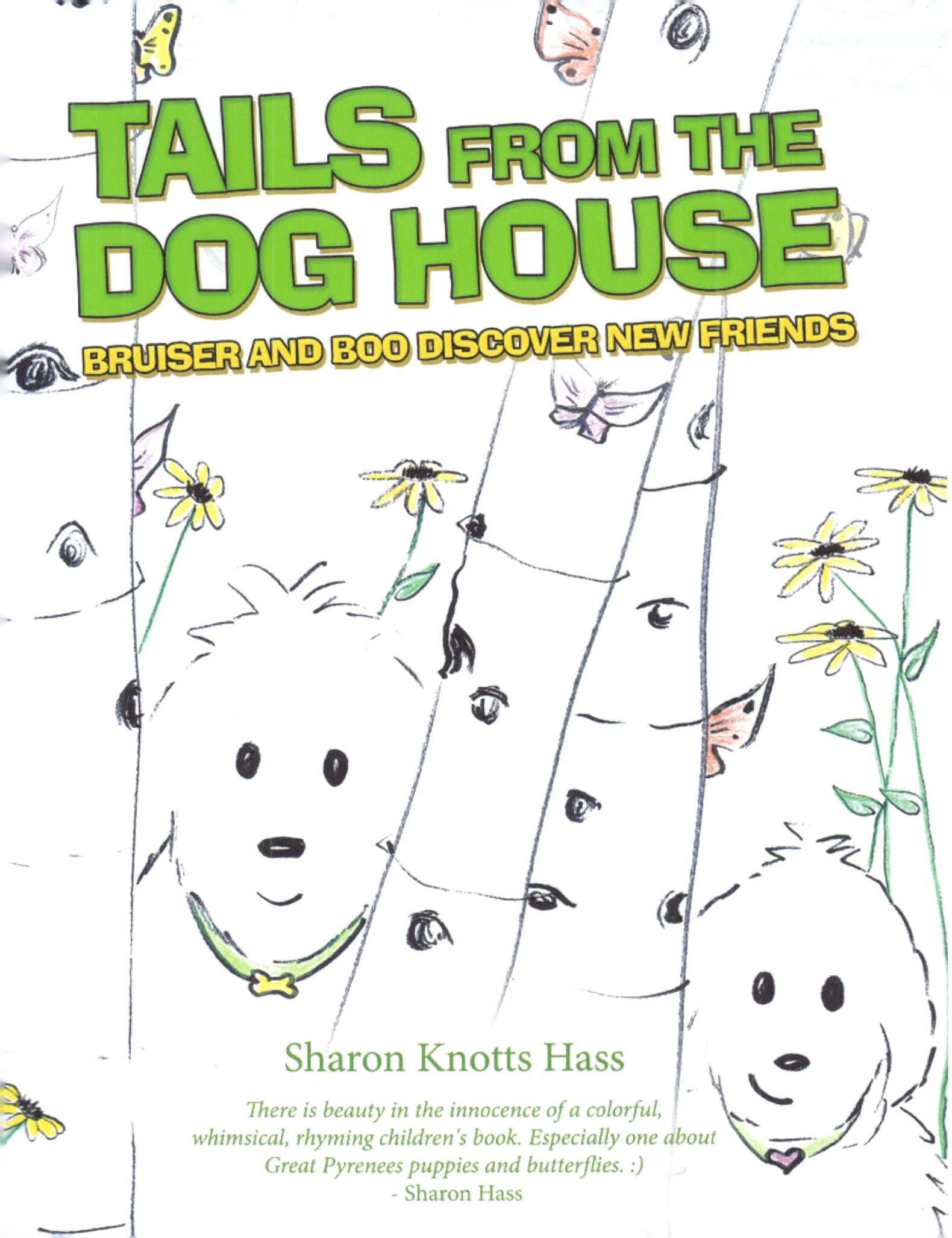

TAILS FROM THE DOG HOUSE

BRUISER AND BOO DISCOVER NEW FRIENDS

Sharon Knotts Hass

There is beauty in the innocence of a colorful,
whimsical, rhyming children's book. Especially one about
Great Pyrenees puppies and butterflies. :)
- Sharon Hass

TAILS FROM THE DOG HOUSE

BRUISER AND BOO DISCOVER NEW FRIENDS

Sharon Knotts Hass

WORKBOOK PRESS LLC
187 E Warm Springs Rd,
Suite B285, Las Vegas, NV 89119, USA

Website: https://workbookpress.com/
Hotline: 1-888-818-4856
Email: admin@workbookpress.com

Ordering Information:
Quantity sales. Special discounts are available on quantity purchases by corporations, associations, and others. For details, contact the publisher at the address above.

Library of Congress Control Number:
ISBN-13:   978-1-958176-22-1 (Paperback Version)
                978-1-958176-23-8 (Digital Version)

REV. DATE: 05/05/2022

Bruiser and Boo are brother and sister Great Pyrenees. Great Pyrenees is one of the most majestic dog breeds. They are very large, snow white, fluffy dogs with big, dark eyes and a cute black nose, often with freckles. Bruiser and Boo are funny, friendly, strong and very smart dogs. They are very protective of their humans. We love them very much. They bring such joy to our lives. I wanted to share them with you. Enjoy!

Tails from the Dog House: Bruiser and Boo Discover New Friends

Bruiser and Boo explore the great outdoors and find a wonderful surprise.

Once upon a warm Spring day, Bruiser and Boo set out to play. They wander down the valley where the green grass grows. There are trees and sunflowers and even a rose.

Oh, the beauty, they cannot believe their eyes! What they see are butterflies of all different colors and size.

Oh, these they love to see. Boo wonders,
"Will one of them come to me?"

Bruiser is waiting to see if they
do. If they do go to Boo.

There they go swirling and fluttering through the air. Bruiser and Boo sit in the field. They watch and stare. The butterflies fly around them without a care. Boo wonders if one will land on her. Will one dare?

Oh, look! There's one now! Boo can't believe this just happened, Wow!

A big, beautiful, blue butterfly has landed on her nose! It won't be long now before it goes.

These butterflies are very busy. Watching them fly makes these curious dogs dizzy. Down through the valley and into the trees. These fantastic creatures go where they please.

Along comes another lovely butterfly, and lands on Boo's nose. It is such a nice comfort, Boo's eyes just close. Bruiser watches close by. He does not get too close, you see, he is quite shy.

Now these beauties need a drink. They gather around a garden sink. Bruiser leads Boo over to watch the amazing butterflies. They watch in wonder as they breath deep sighs.

They are so colorful, dainty and light. Together they are very strong, what a beautiful sight. They seem to float about with such an impressive finesse. The butterflies want to do something special for the dogs to repay them for their kindness.

Up, up they go into the silver lined clouds and the bright, blue sky on a happy adventure. Bruiser and Boo will not ever forget this delightful day, that is for sure.

20

Bruiser and Boo had a great day and now they are enjoying the bright fire's light and the twinkling stars shining so bright, with their friends flying near. They are all resting and planning another day of great cheer with new found friends. This is just how a good day ends.

Until next time, Bruiser and Boo
and the butterflies too, are wishing
you a very good night.☺

24

A special thanks to the crazy, purple haired, goat lady who introduced us to our Great Pyrenees loves, who are Bruiser and Boo. Then there is Rick, the wild goat. (That's a story for another day). What an adventure! ☺

The End

Sharon Knotts Hass has been an animal lover since as far back as she can remember. She can't remember a time in her life without a dog in it. Today she and her family have several pets including Bruiser and Boo.

Sharon likes to include many virtues in her stories. Such as, caring, acceptance, compassion, friendliness and humor to name a few.

She loves her pets and wants to share her stories with you.

BRUISER AND BOO are brother and sister Great Pyrenees, one of the most majestic dog breeds. They are large, snow white, fluffy dogs with big, dark eyes, and a cute black nose, often with freckles. Bruiser and Boo are funny, friendly, strong, and smart dogs.

One day, while exploring the great outdoors, Bruiser and Boo find a wonderful surprise. As the two dogs wander among the green grass, trees, and sunflowers, they discover a variety of butterflies in different sizes and colors. The two dogs enjoy frolicking in the sun with the butterflies.

Tails from the Dog House, a picture book for children, shares the story of an unlikely friendship between newfound friends in nature's beautiful settings.